THE

Peter Meller ZODIAC OF WIT and the Graphic Imagination

by Robert Williams

AD&A MUSEUM
UC SANTA BARBARA
Art, Design & Architecture Museum
University of California Santa Barbara

PREFACE

NO AUTHOR CAN EVER HAVE HAD AS MUCH FUN WRITING A BOOK AS I DID WRITING THIS ONE. I had known Peter Meller as a colleague and had seen that he was a skillful draftsman; he had even given me one of his prints; but it was not until after his death that I realized what an extraordinary graphic artist he had been. Asked to write his obituary, I went to interview his daughter Judit and her husband John Moore. In the midst of discussing Peter's life and character, they showed me two boxes of his work. I marveled at its quality and interest, and when I asked whether there were any more, I was shown a whole room full of such boxes, stacked floor to ceiling, then the garage, where there were shelves full of even larger boxes, and then the big storage shed in the backyard, where there was at least as much material as I had already seen. I quickly decided that all this work needed to be looked at, and in some cases stored more carefully, so I began to go through every box, one at a time. The process took months, but it never felt like work: I turned to each new box with the anticipation of a child opening a Christmas present.

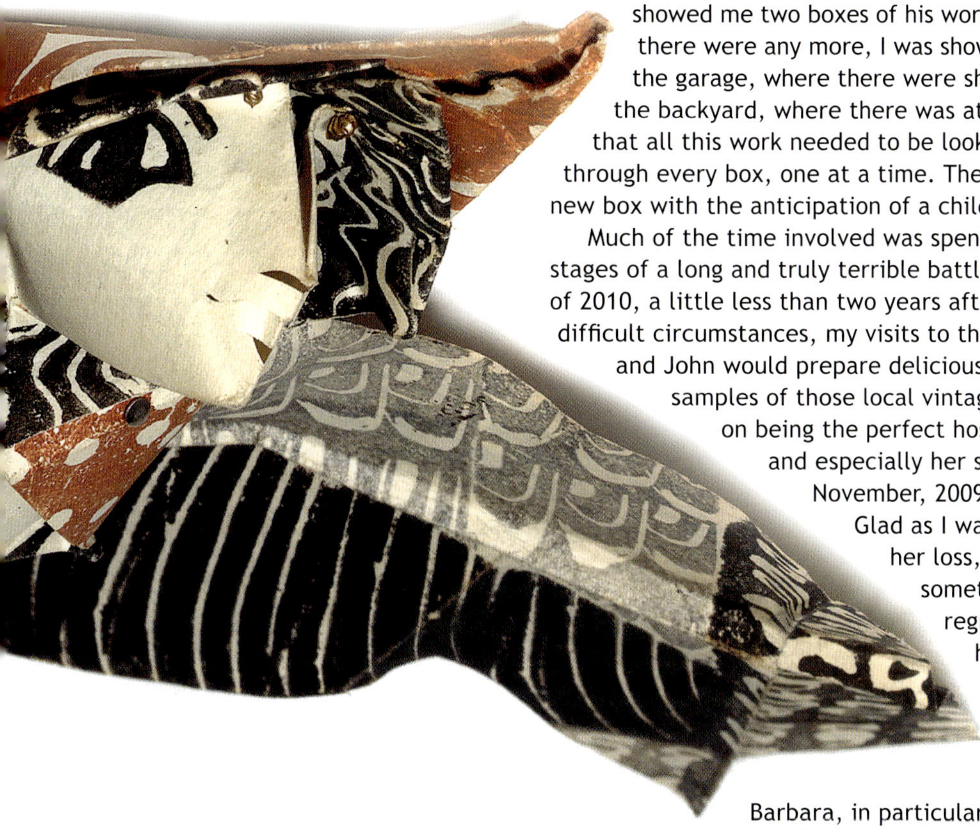

Much of the time involved was spent in the company of Judit and John. Judit was already in the last stages of a long and truly terrible battle with cancer, to which she finally succumbed at the beginning of 2010, a little less than two years after her father's death. She was only sixty years old. Despite the difficult circumstances, my visits to the house were always enjoyable: while they could manage it, Judit and John would prepare delicious multicourse lunches in the Continental style, complete with samples of those local vintages that had passed John's high standards of quality. Judit insisted on being the perfect hostess; she maintained her poise, her appetite for conversation, and especially her sense of humor, right to the end. I finished the text of this book in November, 2009, and John was able to read it to her in the last weeks of her life. Glad as I was that she saw the project reach even that stage of completion, her loss, and the fact that she is not here to see the finished version, is something that—for myself as for John—will always be a cause of bitter regret. Still, the courage and self-possession with which she faced her illness and the selflessness with which John cared for her are things I feel deeply privileged to have witnessed and will never forget.

In addition to Judit and John, I am grateful to other friends of Peter's who shared their stories and insights: in Santa Barbara, in particular, the late Alfred Moir, Régine Astier, Irma Cavat, Ulrich and Ulrike Keller, Fikret Yegul, and Diane Favro; in London, Mári Meller and Caroline Elam; in Budapest, Szilvia Bodnár, Teréz Gerszi, János Szilagyi, and Zsuzsa and Tibor Frank. Jeff Souther and Christine Thomas gave me much needed help with Peter's Greek, Paul Hernadi with his Hungarian.

I am grateful to the staff of the Art, Design & Architecture Museum of the University of California, Santa Barbara, who have enthusiastically supported the realization of a comprehensive exhibition of Peter's work and the publication of this book to accompany it. Elyse Gonzales, Curator of Exhibitions, was the first to take an interest in the project, and Susan Lucke, the Registrar, was indispensible in keeping the entire process running smoothly. The Acting Director of the Museum, Bruce Robertson, gave me much useful advice and practical help along the way. Together with Leslie Gray at the University's Development Office, he saw the fundraising to successful conclusion. I am grateful to the students of my undergraduate seminar in museum studies, as well, who helped with the preparation of the exhibition: their enthusiasm for the project has been a real joy to witness, since in it I can see my old colleague working his charm from beyond the grave to fascinate and inspire a new generation of students.

I would also like to extend a special thanks to those whose generous support has enabled this book to be published: Suzanne Duca, Matthew Moore, Robert Light, Mara and Walter Kohn, Roxanne and James Mattinson, Sara and Walter Gelb, Muriel and John Ridland, and Régine Astier. Finally, thanks to Dana Levy and Tish O'Connor of Perpetua Press for taking care to produce the kind of book, which, in the elegance and playfulness of its design, beautifully transmits the spirit of Peter's work.

The title of this book, as some of its readers will recognize, comes from Sir Phillip Sidney's *Defense of Poesy*, published in 1595, the first major treatise on poetics in the English language. Discussing the way in which poetry involves both the imitation of nature and the exercise of imagination, Sidney writes that the poet "goeth hand in hand with nature, not enclosed within the narrow warrant of her gifts, but ranging freely only within the zodiac of his own wit." This Renaissance conception of creativity, of the mind of the artist as a universe unto itself, seems to me perfectly to express the nature of Peter's approach to his work.

Robert Williams

THE ART OF PETER MELLER
AN INTRODUCTION

PETER MELLER MADE HIS CAREER AS A SCHOLAR, A PROFESSOR OF THE HISTORY OF ART, and was well known among his colleagues for his erudition and insight. He was also an artist. When he died in 2008, at the age of 85, he left behind thousands of drawings and prints, a graphic oeuvre of remarkable size, as well as of distinctive character, brilliance, and charm. His work had been exhibited a few times in and around Santa Barbara, California, where he spent the last half of his life; he sold some prints and gave many away as gifts. Only his family and closest friends had any idea how much time and energy he devoted to his art, and his achievement can only now begin to be appreciated.

In introducing his work, this book can do little more than hint at its range and depth of interest. Peter's scholarly character is everywhere apparent in his images, and some of his more recondite subjects may require explanation, but no book about those images should burden the reader in such a way as to detract from their immediate visual appeal. This essay aims to be as succinct and, as it were, transparent as possible, to provide a brief overview of Peter's life, his preferred techniques, and his favorite themes, and thus to give the reader everything needed to begin a rewarding engagement with his work. The intrinsic quality of that work—its marvelous combination of simplicity and sophistication, acuity and lyricism, playfulness and depth—will continue to fascinate, edify, and delight long after the first encounter.

LIFE

Peter was born in Budapest in 1923. He belonged to a large, prosperous, and cultivated family, Jewish on his father's side, Catholic on his mother's. His father, Dezsö, was an architect and the friend of several of the city's leading avant-garde artists; his paternal uncle, Simon, was an eminent art historian and collector who had served in the years around the first world war as the director of the department of prints and drawings at the Museum of Fine Arts. Peter attended a distinguished school, the Piarist Gymnasium, excelling at the study of Greek and Latin. He also drew and painted: a self-portrait, made with gouache at the age of fifteen, dated 22 August 1938 (fig.1), reveals an already highly developed artistic personality. The structure of the head is suggested with economy and assurance; at the same time, there is a restlessness and impatience in the handling of the paint. In addition to precocious skill, the picture attests a strong-willed commitment to spontaneity as an artistic value, a commitment that would be sustained through all his subsequent work.

At the University of Budapest, Peter continued his studies of classical literature as well as the history of art. Among his teachers was Károly Kerényi, a renowned specialist in the study of ancient myth. Kerényi encouraged his students to think of myths in modern, existential terms, as representing archetypal characters and universal human dilemmas; his influence would have furthered whatever inclination Peter may already have possessed to see the world in terms of recurrent types and situations. Such an orientation is evident in Peter's approach to the history of art, but also the way he looked at life in general and thus his practice as an artist. It sharpened and deepened his appreciation of the human comedy. Kerényi must have had a high regard for his student's intellectual abilities: he invited Peter to participate in an exclusive discussion group that met on Friday evenings.

Civilized as it was, the world into which Peter was born was also full of deadly menace. The Hungarian government tried to maintain a degree of independence from Germany, to which it was formally allied,

<<<< 1. *Self-Portrait*, gouache on paper, dated 22 August 1938

but Nazi sympathizers were numerous and became increasingly powerful in the late '30s and early '40s. On his way to and from school, Peter had to take care to avoid agents of the Hungarian fascist party, the Arrow Cross. He was able to continue his studies during most of the war, but when German troops occupied Hungary in the spring of 1944, it became necessary to go into hiding. He and his immediate family escaped the deportations, but seventeen members of his father's extended family perished in the Holocaust. His older brother, Andrew, who had been pressed into military service, survived the war only to be picked up on the streets of Budapest by the Red Army shortly after the end of hostilities, then sent to Russia, where, condemned as a "fascist collaborator," he died within a few years.

At the end of the war, Peter completed his studies and married Edina Stromer, whom he had met while in hiding from the Germans. He spent the academic year 1947-8 at the Hungarian Academy in Rome engaged in art-historical research. After his return to Budapest, he took a position as curator of the modern sculpture collection at the Museum of Fine Arts, taught art history at the Academies of Fine Arts and Applied Arts, and learned to negotiate the sinister absurdities of a Communist regime he quickly grew to detest. Once ordered by his superiors to remove some pictures by El Greco from display because they represented decadent Western individualism, Peter successfully argued that they should remain on display precisely because they represented decadent Western individualism.

2. Peter at the Trevi Fountain, 1962

Edina gave birth to a daughter, Judit, in 1949. Partly motivated by the desire to make a little extra money, Peter started translating ancient literature into Hungarian: Greek lyric poetry, satyr plays, and epigrams from the *Greek Anthology*, as well as Latin verse. He began the ambitious project of translating the great philosophical poem of Lucretius, *De Rerum Natura* (*On the Nature of Things*), but did not complete it. These translations are poetic achievements in their own right, adapting the lyrical potential of his native language to the various ancient meters with great skill and imagination. Peter would go on to compose Hungarian verse of his own, in the form of epigrams to his images, affectionate parodies of the ancient models he knew so well. Like a Renaissance humanist, he occasionally composed original verse in Latin. He was a poet, in other words, as well as a scholar and artist, and his literary habit of mind had a deep influence on both his scholarship and his art.

In his spare time, Peter sang in a choral group that specialized in the technically difficult music of the late Middle Ages and Renaissance. He also continued to draw and paint, and created designs for scarves, belts, and jewelry. He and Edina enjoyed hosting dinners, and would do their best, even in the period of austerity that followed the war, to prepare memorably sumptuous meals.

Edina died in 1953. A couple of years later, Peter married Mária (Mári) Kálmán, also an art-historian. Like many of their compatriots, they were devastated by the failure of the Hungarian Revolution in 1956, and soon after the brutal Soviet suppression began, they made plans to escape. Attempting to cross over into Austria on foot in the middle of the night, they were captured and briefly imprisoned: released with a stern warning to return to Budapest, they simply made another—this time, successful—effort to flee. Judit, who was seven, always remembered the way her father pressed her hand as they lay side by side in a snowy ditch while a border patrol on skis scanned the surrounding woods with flashlights.

Having given all their money to the guides who helped them escape, Peter and his family arrived in Vienna with next to nothing. Sympathetic colleagues arranged for them to stay in some rooms of the Kunsthistorisches Museum for a few months until a more regular living situation could be found. In a letter written shortly after his arrival in Vienna to his colleague and lifelong friend, János Szilagy, back in Budapest, Peter expressed his pleasure and excitement at having made his way to freedom: he looked forward both to the possibility of unrestricted travel and to opportunities that would allow him to pursue his scholarship. Because permanent academic positions were hard to come by, however, and especially hard to get if one were an émigré, Peter had to take a series of temporary and part-time appointments, interspersed with research fellowships and grants. He moved his family to Florence in 1958, where they remained for a decade, although his academic commitments often involved long periods away. To supplement their income, he and Mári made jewelry. A photo of Peter, taken at the Trevi Fountain in Rome in 1962, captures his intensity and sensitivity, as well as his understated but acute sense of style (fig. 2).

In 1968, he was invited to the University of California, Santa Barbara, as a visiting professor; the following year he was offered a permanent position. He regretted having to leave Europe—and especially to give up on his dream of establishing a permanent home in Italy—but the prospect of financial security was welcome after years of living from one job to the next. He would return to Europe regularly on short trips connected with his research, and even returned several times to Hungary. Still, as anyone who has experienced it knows, life in Italy is infinitely more than the sum of its moments, and intermittent visits offer nothing like the cumulative effect of its more habitual sway.

Something of an exile, therefore, always carefully dressed in jacket and tie, with a rather formal, old-world sense of courtesy and a charming accent, Peter began his adjustment to Southern California. His lectures were popular: students found them impressively learned, thought-provoking, and entertaining. His classes attracted many adult members of the local community: mature auditors often detected a current of sly humor beneath the serious surface of the lectures and wondered whether most of it was not lost on students too young to appreciate it.

As a boy Peter had collected mineral specimens in the mountains of Transylvania; now he could often be seen on the beach, adding to his collection of sea shells. Mári, unable to accept her new surroundings, returned to Europe before long. Judit, who had been trained as a conservator of paintings in Florence, worked in Los Angeles, first at the Los Angeles County Museum of Art, then at the J. Paul Getty Museum, where she was among the first employees to set up the conservation studio. She remained close to her father throughout his life. Upon retiring from teaching in 1994, Peter moved with Judit and her husband, John Moore, a professor of Political Science at UCSB, to a serene hilltop house outside the nearby village of Solvang and was thus able to spend his remaining years in surroundings similar to the rural Tuscany he loved (fig. 3).

3. Peter in retirement, Santa Barbara, c. 1995

As a scholar, Peter specialized in the art of Renaissance Italy. His approach drew upon a range of methods prevalent at the time of his training: like many art historians of his generation, he was attracted to the work of Erwin Panofsky and his student, Edgar Wind. Their emphasis on recurrent themes in the art of the Renaissance, and especially on themes and ideas derived from ancient literature and thought, appealed to Peter's training in the classics and resonated with Kerényi's approach to myth. Yet Peter's interests were wide ranging. He made his reputation with essays on especially complex, elusive figures such as Leonardo da Vinci and Giorgione. He was fascinated by the transmission of forms and styles across cultures and in how, during the Renaissance, the graphic arts contributed to that process. Much of his best work is on portraiture. He seems to have inherited his interest in small-scale bronze sculpture from his uncle Simon, who published a book on German Renaissance bronzes: Peter eventually became a leading authority on the bronzes of Renaissance Italy, his expertise sought out by dealers and collectors until the very last days of his life. A good indication of the range of his interests and erudition is the fact that one of his best-known essays—published after his retirement and only at the repeated urging of colleagues—is entitled "Manet in Italy," and concerns the way in which a pioneering modernist responded to the art of Antiquity and the Renaissance. Beyond its insights into Manet, it offers a glimpse—revealing for the understanding of Peter's own art—of what he thought a modern artist might learn from the art of the past.

4. *Ovid in Exile*, marker

MATERIALS AND METHODS

Peter usually began by making small, very rapid drawings in pencil. These rarely depict persons or objects physically present in front of him; rather, they are imaginative projections, distillations of past experiences with a strong dose of fantasy. Working from the imagination made it easier for him to create a coherent graphic idea, to achieve clarity in the relation of form to content. The facile spontaneity evident in these drawings only comes with years of practice, and it reflects an understanding of drawing as a performing art. The great vase painters of ancient Greece were able to render forms freehand with a line of unerring precision and grace; the effect of lifelikeness that their figures achieve has as much to do with the innate vitality of the line as with its descriptive accuracy (fig. 5). During the Italian Renaissance, skill at drawing (*disegno*) was understood to involve not only the artist's ability to copy what he saw but also to project his intellectual and emotional engagement with what he saw, and thus to endow the resulting image with something of his own life. For the Renaissance masters, as for the Ancients before them, the performative element is essential to art's purpose and meaning, and it plays an equally important role in some forms of modern art. Peter had a deep understanding of this tradition, and its assumptions are implicit in his approach to all his work.

5. *Muse*, Greek white-ground lekythos, c. 445 BCE, Staatliche Antikensammlung, Munich

In drawings such as *Mermaid Combing Her Hair* (fig. 6), *Man and Bulb* (fig. 20), or *Youth with a Book* (fig. 69), the texture of the individual lines show how quickly the pencil was moved over the sheet, and the way in which the lines relate to each other suggests a very rapid process of composition, with each line responding to the one put down just before. The result is a rhythmically animated whole, a complete and intrinsically graphic thought. In *Youth with a Book*, for instance, that thought consists primarily of the relationship between the figure's tousled hair and the pages of the book. In *Old Man with Folded Hands* (fig. 7), the empty whiteness of the paper has been integrated into the composition and thus mobilized for expressive effect. Drawings such as *Pan* (fig. 70) and *Very Old Woman* (fig. 72) display more varied use of the pencil: the first shows energy and incisiveness; the second is built up with lines very gently applied and intentionally smudged to create a delicate shadow. In *Bureaucrat* (fig. 71), on the other hand, shading has been created by peremptorily dragging the side of the pencil point or graphite stick over the original outlines. The result is an overall greyness suggestive of complacent mediocrity: the Italian word *grigiore*, from *grigio*, the word for "grey," means "dullness."

Peter also developed great facility in drawing with marking pens, sometimes using them to enhance pencil sketches, as in *Man Lighting a Pipe* (fig. 74). Thick-pointed black pens helped him quickly set down arrangements of forms in light and dark, but he also liked to use a fine-pointed pen to add details and finishing touches. In a small sketch of a *Mermaid with a Mirror* (fig. 73) he defined the form negatively by rapidly filling in the surrounding space with a thick-pointed marker, then, using a fine-pointed one, made a few deft touches to complete the articulation of face and body. In *Gypsy Mother* (fig. 75), the figure is drawn in black to set it off against the white ground, but it is enlivened by patterns added with a fine-tipped silver marker; a simple, yet striking border emphasizes the decorative effect. More dramatic than decorative, yet also indicative of Peter's thinking in terms of graphic contrast, is a drawing of two male figures locked in hand-to-hand combat (fig. 76): the one on the left is black, defined by exposed areas of white paper surrounding it; the other, white, is set against a black field quickly created with a marker. The white figure is skeletal and seems to represent death: he attacks the other, who attempts to hold him off with a stiff right arm. The elemental graphic contrast between white and black is thus made to express the elemental existential struggle between death and the will to live.

Although most of Peter's images involve human figures, he was responsive to all aspects of nature and found distinctive means to express it. His drawings of animals, for instance, resemble caricatures, simplifying but also humanizing the creature, so that the viewer has the impression of suddenly coming face to face with a distinctive and amusing personality, as a reader does in the fables of Aesop. The drawing of a *Lemur* (fig. 78), apparently inspired by a photograph, began with thin brown lines over which Peter made rapid, energetic additions in black marker. The *Hedgehog* (fig. 77) gets much of its character from the contrast between its simple, semicircular contour and the way in which the texture of its fur is suggested by the delicate feathering of the black marker and repeated strokes of the silver marker.

A drawing of parsley stalks, labeled in a printed version with the Italian name of the herb, *Prezzemolo*

6. ***Mermaid Combing Her Hair*, pencil**

7. ***Old Man with Folded Hands*, pencil**

(fig. 9), is one of the few drawings made in front of the object it depicts. Again, it seems to have started as a pencil sketch, to which additions were made with black and silver marker. A rapid, simplified notation captures the look of real parsley leaves, but also brims with lyrical vitality, reminding a viewer familiar with Renaissance art of Leonardo's botanical studies (fig. 8). A forest scene, an illustration (fig. 79) of an episode in the Hungarian classic *János Vitéz* (*John the Valiant*), is an even more brilliant demonstration of marker technique. The trunks of the trees have been laid in with extremely quick, bold strokes, resulting in streaks suggestive of the rough texture of bark. A second marker was used to fill in some branches, as well as the tiny figure of János, disappearing behind a tree; a third, nearly dried-out, to fill in the ground around the path. To create leaves, Peter used rubber stamps he had made, but then also added leaves in thin-pointed black and silver marker. With its combination of power and delicacy, the image taps a deep, instinctive, lyrical response to nature; it suggests the fearsomeness of the forest but also its fascination and beauty.

8. Leonardo da Vinci, *Plant Study* (*"Star of Bethlehem"*) Royal Library, Windsor

Peter recorded many of his first ideas with brush and ink wash or watercolor; like markers, these materials allowed him to organize patterns of light and dark over an entire sheet with only a few movements of the hand, to set down a graphic idea as quickly as possible, with both boldness and nuance. In *Woman Hanging Laundry* (fig. 80), the figure's weighty form is emphasized by the basket on the ground next to her, but it is also defined by its contrast with the clothes gently waving in the breeze. Although she is characterized as earthy and voluptuous, her acute sidelong glance at the viewer gives her another dimension and the image as a whole a mysterious suggestiveness. A portrait of *Béla Bartók* (fig. 81), one of a series that Peter made of famous men and women, is much more finished, yet it retains the freshness of something executed quickly. Copied from a well-known photograph of the composer, it brilliantly translates the pattern of light recorded in the photograph into a play of contrasts in paint. Something of the sheer intelligence with which this translation is made communicates itself even to viewers with no knowledge of watercolor technique, subtly enhancing the characterization of an unusually intelligent man.

Drawing, whether with pencil, marker, or brush, was only the beginning: Peter's drawings served as points of departure for further graphic development. His usual practice was to photocopy the original, then rework the photocopy, making adjustments and additions. The reworked version would then be photocopied as the "definitive" form of the image, but the process of revision might be repeated many times before a satisfactory conclusion was reached. This method allowed the work to develop in stages, each rapid, thus to retain spontaneity while also producing a provisionally "finished" result. It resembles the procedure of a musician who, over time, casually improvises a series of variations on his own original theme.

The obvious advantages of photocopying are that it is fast and easy. That Peter did not work in any of the traditional graphic media—engraving, etching, lithography—certainly has a great deal to do with the fact that they are slow and labor-intensive. Photocopying also allows for greater flexibility: the artist does not have to efface the first version of an image in the process of refining it, but can easily save each stage in the developmental process, so that each can potentially become the starting point for a new and different train of thought. Another attraction would have been its novelty, the fact that it was not a traditional graphic medium. The electrophotographic process on which it depends was invented in 1938, but photocopying did not become commercially viable or widespread until the 1960s. As a commonplace, déclassé form of graphic reproduction, it exists in a fundamentally ironic relation to traditional techniques; that relation becomes a source of meaning, and especially of humor, in many of Peter's images.

An ironic humor is also implicit in his use of common correction fluid, together with its applicator, a miniature parody of an artist's paintbrush. In some cases, correction fluid is indeed used to correct, that is to efface or "white-out" unwanted marks, but in others it is a means of adding to the image; it becomes an instrument of expression. In the *Allegorical Figure* (fig. 82) and *Capriccio* (*Caprice*, fig. 83) for instance, it is used in a way that brilliantly complements the handling of the marker. In *The Ill-Tempered Clavier* (fig. 84) it is used to create the curls in the musician's peruke and lace collar, a droll touch entirely in keeping with the humor of the image as a whole.

Sometimes the transition from drawing to finished print was simple: the printed version of *Béla Bartók*, for instance, involved no change except addition of the label. But if the watercolor shows Peter translating a photograph into another medium, it is clear that he also saw that translation itself as provisional, a stage

9. *Prezzemolo (Parsley)*, pencil and marker

in a process, that he was thinking of the black-and-white image all along, thinking graphically, even when painting in color. More typical is *A Woman on a Rock in the Sea*: an energetic marker sketch (fig. 85) was evidently photocopied and the photocopy subjected to a single, equally spirited but wholly different sort of intervention, in which details were added to the woman's body and to the waves surrounding her before the image was copied again to create the final version (fig. 86).

A watercolor of *Rooftops* (fig. 87) captures with impressionistic immediacy the picturesque jumble of an Italian village seen from a high vantage point: as a graphic and poetic thought it is complete in itself, yet Peter improvised on it by photocopying it, then going over the photocopied version with a fine-tipped white or silver marker to create a delicate network of lines representing the roof tiles. This addition, with its nervous energy, perfectly complements the simple masses of the original watercolor to produce an even more complete and satisfying image (fig. 88). Just as his forest scene expresses a powerful and complex feeling before nature, his image of an Italian village, charged with a poet's sense of enchanted possibility—of a

10. *Dead Harpy*, pen and ink

hundred interesting sights waiting to be seen, a hundred intriguing encounters waiting to happen—becomes a symbol of the mystery and infinite possibility of human life.

Usually Peter's working process was complex. The original line drawing, in pen and ink, of a *Dead Harpy* (fig. 10) is one of his most striking images: harpies are traditional symbols of predatory women—and figure as such frequently in Peter's work—but in this instance, the harpy is a victim and object of pity. This design went through several stages, involving addition and correction (fig. 11). Broad-tipped black marker in the wings and tail give weight and create a stark contrast with the white sheet; at the same time, they are relieved by lines in white pencil articulating the feathers. A grey marker has been used to give the face the color of death, while the breasts have been worked up with correction fluid, poignantly emphasizing the nearness of voluptuousness to vulnerability. The exact configuration of the claws has been achieved through careful addition, but also by "whiting-out" unwanted parts before photocopying the definitive version. The reworked image may sacrifice something of the spontaneity and lyrical delicacy of the original ink sketch, but gains in the force and depth of the feelings it evokes.

The image of *Pandora* is an example of how complex the process could be. The figure seems to have evolved from an earlier composition illustrating the myth of Orpheus and Eurydice. At some point the pose, with its elegant, yet expressive twist of the body, indicating a sudden change of mind or moment of regret, must have suggested an entirely different story. An unusually labored drawing in pencil and marker (fig. 89) became the basis for an even more labored reworking with correction fluid: the head and body were modeled differently, and the vase, with its escaping cloud of evils, was added (fig. 90). Here again, the final version may lose something in spontaneity: Peter chose to suppress Pandora's open eye, and carefully adjusted the relation of the raised hand to the face. These changes emphasize her incomprehension: though she suspects that she has made a mistake, she can have no idea of just how fateful a mistake it is. Peter obviously knew the earliest accounts of the story in the writings of the ancient Greek mythographer Hesiod: he renders the container as a large jar (*pithos*) and does not follow the later mistranslation by showing it as a box (*pyxis*). He is also faithful to the spirit of Hesiod's interpretation, in which Pandora, the first woman, is a figure of irresistible beauty while also being responsible for all the miseries that afflict mankind. In Peter's hands she becomes, like the Eve of the Old Testament, a symbol of the radical ambivalence of sexual desire, and the conflicted feelings that her story arouses may explain the unusually intensive reworking to which he subjects her image.

11. *Dead Harpy*, photocopy reworked with pencil, marker, and correction fluid

The brilliant marker drawing of *A Seated Girl in Classical Dress*, quite perfect in black and white (fig. 91), became the basis for variations in color (fig. 92), illustrating another of Peter's favorite methods of improvisation: the original design was photocopied onto colored paper and the copied version then enhanced with additions in pastel and correction fluid. There are at least two painted versions of this print; others are reproduced and varied in the same manner numerous times. Peter's use of color is always restrained; it never overwhelms the essentially graphic nature of the design. Significantly, the hand-colored sheets are all printed on colored paper to begin with, so that color has been introduced into the graphic arrangement from the start. Only such additions are then made as will create a new graphic interest. In the image of the *Old Pope* (fig. 93) he picks out the jewels on the tiara with touches just like those used for the whites of the eyes; the barely visible addition of brown to the lips completes the enhanced effect of ghastliness. In the *Son of William Tell* (fig. 68) the addition of white to the eyes adds both to the expression of fear and its comic inflection. The use of other muted colors is intentionally reminiscent of old-fashioned popular prints.

Another of Peter's favorite techniques was to create designs that he then photocopied in negative, so that white forms became black and black forms white. One example from among the hundreds of such images that he made represents the face of an old woman. To realize, when looking at the original drawing (fig. 94), that Peter was calculating how it would look with the values reversed (fig. 95)—thinking in negative, so to speak—is to recognize how intense and highly developed his graphic imagination was. He cultivated a distinctive style of drawing for such images, and the resulting prints have a distinctive look: he tended to reserve this technique for subjects of an ugly, grotesque, or disturbing nature, and the prints are often startling and hallucinatory in a way that enhances their expressive effect.

Yet another favorite technique involved painting with correction fluid on black paper. These images are usually very small: the *Death of Orpheus* (fig. 12) is about three inches square; *Worship of the Golden Calf* (fig. 13), at four and a half by six inches, is one of the largest. So concentrated are they that when photocopied in larger form they lose none of their impact, yet most were made small in order to be reproduced on a small scale. Again, a particular style was developed for them. The contrast of white and black possesses inherent graphic interest; it might even be described as the foundation of all graphic interest: the challenge of composing such pictures seems to have prompted Peter to strive for the exemplary graphic virtues of simplicity, concentration, and balance. They thus have a strongly classical quality, close in spirit to Greek vase painting, even when their subject matter is not taken from ancient myth or history. Though energetically and spontaneously painted, they sometimes also show careful correction. The *Death of Orpheus* contains a change, or *pentimento*, in the lower left corner, where the extended leg has been deleted with black marker, so that the composition achieves better balance and integration. In the *Worship of the Golden Calf*—a meticulously calculated image of raucous abandon—many of the outlines and most of

12. *Death of Orpheus,* correction fluid on black paper

13. *Worship of the Golden Calf,* correction fluid and marker on black paper

14: Mounted transparencies in plastic frames with magnetized backing

the details of the faces have been added over the white paint in fine-pointed black marker. The result is a design in which energy and humor have been combined with perfect clarity and formal discipline.

Peter sometimes drew with black marker directly onto sheets of clear plastic. The forms were usually set down quickly and roughly as silhouettes; their internal articulation, together with any corrections and additions, was then made in the photocopied versions. More frequently, he photocopied designs onto transparent sheets of plastic. The resulting image could then be treated in a variety of ways. The sheet itself could be reworked by scratching off excess ink with a needle or knife. It could also be photocopied, in turn, against different backgrounds. Although Peter most often opted for plain backgrounds, he also created many more complex ones, usually collages made from variously patterned sheets. Putting the principal motif on a sheet of plastic enabled him to test different backgrounds quickly and easily. By simply turning the sheet over, he could reverse the motif.

These plastic sheets could also be mounted against colored backgrounds as finished works. By varying the backgrounds, identical prints could thus be made into one-of-a-kind objects. Peter especially liked to use thin sheets of metallic foil as backgrounds: A beautiful *Mermaid* in correction fluid and white pencil on black paper (fig. 96) was altered, photocopied in negative onto a plastic sheet, and mounted against a piece of gold foil (fig. 97). For the *Head of Apollo* (fig. 99), gold foil with smaller pieces of silver and muted metallic green were used. The complementarity of force and sparkle helps to make these mounted transparencies some of Peter's most beautiful creations.

Peter also painted with correction fluid directly onto transparent pieces of plastic. These images are usually small and could then be photocopied, magnified, against colored backgrounds. Like the paintings on black paper, they have a classical economy and balance, but reveal even greater fluency and assurance in the way they are executed, as is especially evident in the portraits of *Rogier van der Weyden* (fig. 100) and *Albert Einstein* (fig. 101). The portraits of *Pablo Picasso* (fig. 102) and *Samuel Beckett* (fig. 103), on the other hand, have been vigorously reworked with a needle, scraping away areas of correction fluid to create texture and to add power and complexity to the characterization.

Peter used the designs in correction fluid on black paper and transparent plastic to produce several hundred very small "transparencies," each of which he then inserted into a flat plastic frame, attaching a magnetic sheet to the back, so that the result resembles a common refrigerator magnet (fig. 14). The humor implicit in the attempt to elevate such a banal object to the level of art—or to bring art down to the level of the everyday—is obviously related to his playful engagement with the banal technology of photocopying.

Another of Peter's favorite media was stamps, which he designed and carved himself. The images he produced by this means constitute about half of his entire graphic output and represent a truly unique achievement, an artistic language as original as it is expressive and beautiful. Most of the stamps are made from plastic draughtsman's erasers, but he used other common objects, such as the corks of wine bottles and the wheels of toy cars. He preferred a reddish-brown ink, similar to the color Italians call *sanguigno*, which also resembles the color of Greek red-figure vases. The style, too, exemplified, for instance by *Fortuna (*or, to be more precise, *Occasio*; fig. 15), evokes ancient painting, yet it is also modern and informal, almost cartoonlike in its simplicity: it is at once an updating and an affectionate parody of ancient style. Like Peter's use of photocopying, it has an inherent humor, grounded perhaps in the classicist's sense of there being a fundamentally ironic relation between past and present. Much of its appeal derives from the way in which it models such ironic consciousness—demonstrating both grace and wit—and thus its value as an outlook on life.

Some of the stamps represent entire figures, but many are of heads and individual body parts , elements that could be combined in different ways to produce an endless variety of characters. There are also stamps of animals, plants, architectural elements, and other forms. If the rendering of the individual motifs is itself a source of humor, Peter also took obvious delight in combining and recombining them: the process of variation and improvisation is both logical and playful. The images made with stamps are all unique, though Peter usually photocopied the ones he liked best, often reworking the photocopied versions with marker and correction fluid to produce new designs.

Terremoto (*Earthquake*; fig. 18) is a complex composition built up with a variety of small stamps, some of them simple geometric forms repeated so that their juxtaposition suggests real objects. In several places, such as the collapsing wall with windows to the left, Peter has used the same stamp twice, simply turning it upside down to create variety; at the right, he has used another stamp, possibly a rough piece of cork, three

15. *Fortuna* (or *Occasio*) stamped print

times, turning it upside down once to make the repetition less obvious. Several variants of the composition among Peter's papers indicate that he had a great deal of fun experimenting with different arrangements before arriving at the final composition.

Buddhist Monk Going Home (fig. 19) is one of Peter's most inspired works. The figure of the monk was made with a single flat plastic stamp, but the ropes of the ladder were produced using a thin circular object, possibly an old typist's eraser or a thin slice of wine cork. Peter cut a simple pattern of grooves around the rim, then, using a hole in the middle through which he could put a slender shaft of some kind, a nail or a toothpick, created a little wheel. The rim of the wheel was rolled in ink, then rolled on the surface of the paper to produce the continuous pattern of the rope. The rungs of the ladder were then added like hyphens, using another simple little stamp. The mountains in the background were made by first photocopying onto the sheet, very faintly, in brown ink, the torn pieces of a brown paper shopping bag. The use of such humble materials is a source of humor in itself, but the humility also resonates with the subject in a way that is both amusing and deeply endearing. The trial versions of this print among Peter's papers show him adjusting the position, angle, and twist of the ladder, as well as the figure's position on it, each option saying something slightly different about the monk's degree of spiritual liberation from worldly cares.

Given Peter's interest in techniques of visual reproduction, it is not surprising that he was also fascinated by pattern. He created patterns in many ways, but he especially enjoyed generating them out of stamped motifs. In the case of *Apollo and the Muses* (page 7), simple repetition makes a single motif into a new image with a formal logic of its own, a rhythmic embodiment of the idea of art. One of his lovely images of angels (fig. 129), alternating with the simple motif of a column, creates a pattern that he used to make wrapping paper for Christmas presents (fig. 130). Other designs, developed with photocopies, were printed on cloth to make scarves, most of which he gave away as gifts.

In addition to jewelry, Peter also produced some sculpture. Most remarkable, perhaps, are the figures of harpies made from printed and painted sheets of folded paper (page 4-5). Peter intended them not to be hung from strings as mobiles, but to be thrown like paper airplanes, and he spent a great deal of time perfecting their aerodynamic qualities. He was especially concerned that they land and come to rest gracefully.

His most ambitious sculptures are models of imaginary Italian villages, with buildings made out of styrofoam and cardboard, and painted or decorated with printed patterns (fig. 117). The buildings and other elements can be moved at the viewer's whim to create different arrangements, and thus different villages, but Peter thought of them all as variations on a single, archetypal village, which he called "Pisolino," from the Italian word meaning "nap" or "snooze." These sculptures are his most elaborate attempt to capture the fascination of small Italian towns, his sense of their being both humble—"sleepy"—places and microcosms of the human condition. They were all made in California and can thus be understood as a product of nostalgia, of a desire to re-create in miniature an Italy he could no longer possess in reality, but they also represent the process by which he came to grips with the idealized nature of his fascination, with the fact that what he sought was no single place but a state of mind.

Peter never signed his drawings and only occasionally signed his prints. More often he would stamp printed sheets with a monogram consisting of his initials or attach a monogram printed on adhesive paper. Owing to the

17. Opposite: **Assorted rubber stamps >>>>**

16. ***Saint Barbara,*** **rubber stamp and stamped print**

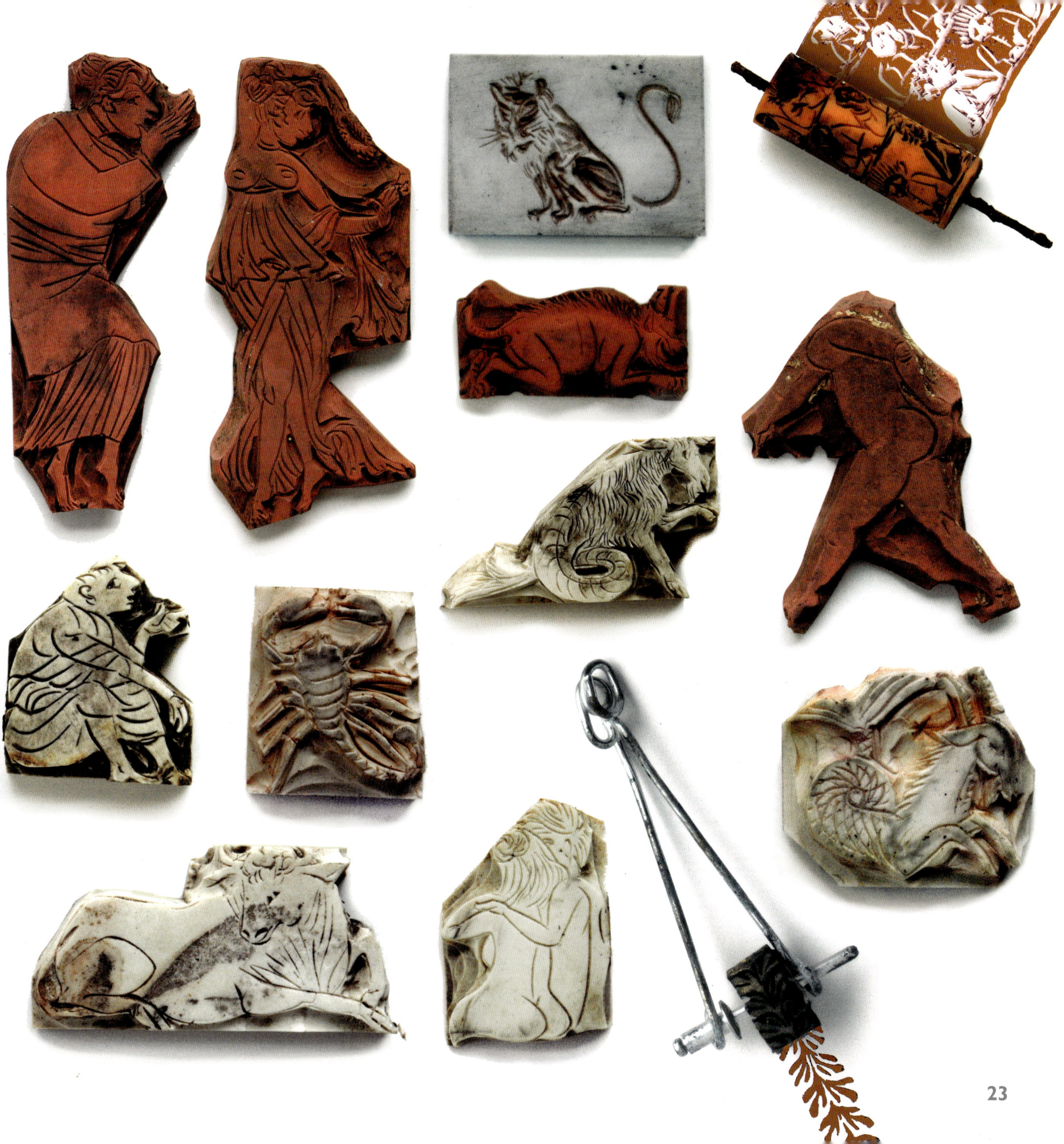

way he worked, and the difficulty of determining where the development of any image ends, it is tempting to suppose that affixing the monogram marks the completion of the creative process. Yet while it usually documents Peter's relative satisfaction with the point to which his work had led him thus far, he often took up a signed or monogrammed sheet to rework yet again, sometimes, to judge from the evidence, many years later. This can make it hard to decide which version of any image is to be regarded as definitive. The existence of numerous copies may offer a clue, but this criterion, too, is not always reliable. Another imperfect indication is paper quality: Peter often tried out his ideas on inexpensive paper, then, when he believed he had arrived at something like a final version, he would photocopy them onto finer-quality, usually heavier paper, but he was not systematic in this practice either. He clearly thought of his drawings as part of the preparatory process and only regarded the prints as finished works: he rarely attached monograms to drawings and never made any attempt to exhibit or sell them.

Peter seldom put dates on his work. Largely on the basis of his sensitivity to fashion, some drawings can be roughly dated to the late 1950s or early '60s, and some drawings and prints from the mid-60s to the mid-70s. In the mid-80s, he dated a group of prints he was preparing for exhibition. As a result, and also because his creative process often involved returning to resume work on old designs, it is hard to ascertain any developmental trajectory over the course of his career.

18. ***Terremoto (Earthquake)***, **stamped print**

19. ***Buddhist Monk Going Home*, stamped print**

THEMES

Like the Renaissance artists he admired, but also like many modern artists, Peter was interested in the variety of human character types, and many of his drawings and prints, images of individuals, can be described as character studies. His own names for them were *tipi* (types) or *caratteri* (characters). Young and old, beautiful and ugly, good and evil, fortunate and unfortunate, they constitute an extended survey of human experience as revealed in both the enduring structures of character and transient emotional states. The idea that art should reflect a comprehensive knowledge of human nature was already well established in ancient times: such knowledge was thought to elevate the poet or painter to the intellectual level of the philosopher. Leonardo wanted the painter to possess "universal" understanding, but a similar ideal, expressed with different words, is also evident in the open-minded receptivity to the world, the combination of "naiveté" and "cosmopolitanism" that the nineteenth-century poet Baudelaire admired in the work of his contemporary, the graphic artist Constantin Guys, and that others have seen at work in artists like Manet, Degas, and Picasso.

Almost none of these images of Peter's were made directly from life. Some may have their origin in specific memories, but most are imaginative inventions: Peter dreamt up characters based on the people he had encountered or read about, or states of being that he had experienced himself, and he sought to give the most vivid possible shape to them, so that his characterizations respond to the demands of graphic formulation. Sometimes they represent faces alone, but often they show the entire body: sensitive as he was to the nuances of facial expression, Peter was just as alert to the ways in which character and emotion are revealed in pose and gesture.

Man with a Bulb (fig. 20), a line drawing that could have taken no more than about ten seconds to make,

20. *Man with a Bulb*, pencil

21. *Old Woman Ironing*, pencil, marker, and correction fluid

22. *Old Tailor*, pencil, marker, and correction fluid

exemplifies the tendency to caricature evident in many of these images: the juxtaposition of bulb and bald head emphasizes the similarity of their forms, but only to create a more marked contrast between the dim-wittedness suggested by the characterization of the man and the object symbolizing intellectual illumination. *Old Man with Folded Hands* (fig. 7), though also a quick line drawing, is entirely different in effect. For all its simplicity, it expresses a complex internal state: "sadness," though perhaps the first word that comes to mind, is an oversimplification; to describe it as a chastely self-negating resignation would perhaps be more accurate. The delicately drawn *Very Old Woman* (fig. 72) creates a sense of fragility that elicits both horror and sympathy, balancing the artist's capacity for objectivity, on the one hand, and compassion on the other.

Two sheets, which seem to have been done at about the same time, representing an *Old Woman Ironing* (fig. 21) and an *Old Tailor* (fig. 22), are among Peter's most charming inventions and show how, in full-figure images, pose and gesture enhance the characterization. Here too, he achieves perfect clarity in the relation of form to content: everything, down to the last detail, seems to be motivated by a single, consistent impulse, so that beyond presenting us with two personalities in a way that is both affectionate and parodic, they demonstrate an overarching intellectual poise, a sovereign comic perspective on life as a whole.

Full-figure compositions also show how the suggestion of movement contributes to the expression of character. A *Pandiramerinaio* (fig. 104)—a vendor of rosemary rolls traditionally sold outside Florentine churches at Eastertime—carries himself with an amusingly inflated sense of his social importance. In contrast, a *Man with Wine Bottles* (fig. 105) shambles along in an uncertain state of sobriety. *Woman with Flowers* (fig. 106) represents a familiar urban type: though the woman has taken care to dress stylishly, she strides forward briskly and distractedly, as if preoccupied, so that one must wonder about the purpose of the flowers she holds.

Girl Before a Mirror (fig. 23), a subject often treated in art since the Renaissance, also has to do with self-consciousness: the girl's posing presupposes her awareness of her beauty, and we are invited to take as much pleasure in the contours of her body as she does in their reflection. *Prancing Woman* (fig. 24), on the other hand, captures a moment of unselfconscious abandon to irresistible joy. The vitality and the humor of the sketch both have their source in the way such an amply proportioned woman is shown romping so energetically: both its persuasiveness and its comic effect are emphasized by the necklace hovering in mid-air. The means involved are so simple that one recognizes the line itself—thick where it describes the woman's hips and breasts, but thinner in her face and hands—to be animated by what can only be described as an intrinsically comic energy.

23. *Girl before a Mirror,* stamped print

24. *Prancing Woman,* pencil and marker

25. ***Pensive Girl,*** **pencil and watercolor**

Pensive Girl (fig. 25), a quick pencil sketch transformed by additions in watercolor, establishes a mood both simple and difficult to describe. The curving pattern of the clothing she wears, or blanket she has wrapped herself in, sets off the roundness of her face, which in turn accentuates the roundness of her eyes, and thus helps to determine her expression. At the same time, the stripes of her wrap work with her fingers to emphasize the position of her hand. Is she wiping away a tear, or just gesturing absent-mindedly? Looking out into our space but not at us, she is absorbed in her own thoughts: we are presented with the fact of her inwardness without being given any clear indication of what she is thinking or feeling. Yet despite its ambiguity, we respond to the mood it creates: perhaps it addresses our own experience of ambiguity, our sense of how it is possible to feel, say, contentedness and anxiety at the same time.

Woman in a Flower-Patterned Shirt (fig. 26) is another psychologically complex image fashioned with simple means: the object against which the figure leans, for instance, was made with a single rolling stamp. The woman looks directly at us, but who is she and what is she thinking? Is she innocent and pure, leaning, perhaps, against a tree, and meeting our glance with naïve curiosity, or a prostitute standing against a wall? The ambiguity is intentional and creates a mood of its own: wholly ordinary yet mysterious, inscrutable yet also vulnerable, the woman elicits our sympathetic attention regardless of who she is.

Artist in a Doorway (fig. 27) would seem to be more straightforward, but it is ambiguous in another way. The artist is represented as a *flaneur*, one who stands apart to observe the urban scene with critical detachment, but his position in a doorway also invites comparison with the prostitute, and like the prostitute, he has wares to offer: with his portfolio beside him, he is on the lookout, not only for new subjects to depict, but also for customers. The fact that Peter could ridicule artistic pretensions so sharply reveals his ability to turn upon and objectify himself; it exposes the hidden rigor of his comic outlook.

26. ***Woman in Flower-Patterned Shirt,*** **stamped print**

27. ***Artist in a Doorway,*** **stamped print**

Peter's interest in human nature is also evident in representations of the interaction between two individuals, images he classified as "couples" (*coppie*). These range from the amusing to the deeply heartwarming, but also explore the darker themes of emotional dependency, domination, submission, and abuse. Some are illustrations of recognizable stories, but most are not. That they often suggest narratives of some kind is an indication that they engage our interest and speak to our experience, yet Peter frequently leaves crucial details unspecified, showing that he is generally less interested in telling stories than in concentrating our attention on their essential emotional content.

The image of a man recoiling from a female singer (fig. 28) was assembled from two drawings, both made with extraordinary speed and economy of means: the man was drawn first; the woman was then sketched on a separate sheet, which was glued to the other in order to create a complete composition. Though assembled from two parts, the result is a graphic unity based on contrast and complementarity. The man's panic, registered in his horizontal movements, is emphasized by being set against the woman, who draws herself

28. *Man and Singing Woman*, pencil, marker and correction fluid

29. ***Elderly Couple***, **photocopy**

up to her full height to emit her high note. The jarring effect of the whole—suggesting that the singer is badly off-key—is emphasized by the juxtaposition of black and white backgrounds. Comical though it is, the man's sudden, spasmodic reaction seems to reveal a deep instinctive fear, an ordinarily suppressed sense of a fundamental incompatibility or antagonism between men and women.

In the wash drawing *Women at a Railing* (fig. 107), the figures are rendered with a minimum of internal modeling, yet the poses of their bodies and their relation to each other are expressive of their ease in each others' presence. We may not be able to overhear their conversation, but we get a clear sense of its intimacy and warmth. In another wash drawing, showing a rather haughty man and an adoring woman (fig. 108), the relation of the two figures is calculated to suggest the contrast but also the mutual dependence of their attitudes: the man needs someone to admire him as much as the woman wants someone to admire. Again, one is struck by the speed and clarity with which a complex idea has been noted down on paper, the way that two figures have been grasped as a single thing, a single pictorial organism, as it were, a single graphic event.

One of Peter's most memorable images shows an elderly couple embracing (fig. 29). The gender of the two figures is uncertain: is it a man and wife, or two sisters, or a mother and daughter? The answer hardly matters: the whole interest of the work lies in the simple contrast between the grimness of the faces and the tenderness of the embrace. Starkly rendered in black and white, without any middle tones, and in a style

30. ***Man Courting a Woman,*** **marker, correction fluid, pasted overlay**

31. ***Unequal Couple,*** **photocopy**

32. ***Mother and Child***, **photocopy**

33. ***Mother and Child***, **photocopy**

similar to that of the early twentieth-century expressionist Kathe Kollwitz, these characters seem to have weathered unspeakable hardship and pain, yet their love for one another endures, immovable as a mountain.

Many of the *coppie* depict lovers. In *A Man Courting a Woman* (fig. 30), the relationship between the two figures has been very carefully calculated. Peter actually glued a second drawing of the man's body onto the sheet, leaving the original head and hands exposed. Now seen just slightly more in profile, rather than with his back turned as in the first version, he stands in more awkward relation to the woman but also in a different, closer relation to us: we are invited to laugh at his shyness but also to sympathize with him. The woman's twisting pose registers an ambivalence on her part, a combination of interest and skepticism, that answers to the conflict of feelings at work in the man. Here too, sympathy and objectivity support each other: sensitive as he is to all the nuances of the encounter, Peter describes the scene with the acuity of a zoologist observing some mating ritual in the animal kingdom. Like the *Old Woman Ironing* and *Old Tailor*, the result points beyond itself to an overarching comic outlook on life as a whole.

A drawing with additions in watercolor, marker, and correction fluid, showing a seated girl and her lover (fig. 109) became an object of further improvisation when photocopied onto colored paper (fig. 110). The hopeless mismatch between the impassivity of the girl and the desperate attentiveness of the boy acquires a morbid cast in the reworked version but it retains its humor. *Unequal Couple* (fig. 31) presents us with an even more unbalanced relationship, as disturbing as it is funny.

Peter's depictions of the relationships between children and adults are also very sensitive: *Mother and Child* (fig. 32) beautifully contrasts the inert, protective mass of the woman's body with the lively movements of her little infant. A rather less idealized image of motherhood shows a child hanging from its mother's hair (fig. 33). More enigmatic and poetically suggestive is a stamped image, classified among Peter's files under the title *Gathering Chestnuts* (fig. 111): the intimacy of a little boy and a mature woman, possibly his governess but most probably his mother, is represented with a sensitivity that suggests some basis in Peter's own childhood experience.

The images of antagonistic pairings range from the relatively gentle, such as *Old Man Scolding a Boy* (fig. 112), to the brutally violent. In *Two Men Arguing* (fig. 113), the narrative is unclear but the unequal and abusive nature of the relationship is obvious. We suspect that we are witnessing torture. Peter had plenty of experience living in fear of such treatment, and its psychological effects were permanent. Radiant as his comic vision was, and much as he privileges images of love, the dark side of human nature was always present to his imagination and he used his work to counter and exorcise its influence.

A survey of Peter's *coppie* might perhaps also include his images of human figures with animals: *Girl*

34. ***Girl with a Unicorn*, stamped print**

35. ***Hero Resting*, photocopy**

with a Unicorn (fig. 34) and *Hero Resting* (fig. 35) are both situated in the realm of myth and legend. More modern and less pastoral are a pair of prints that emphasize, albeit amusingly, the stressful aspects of inter-species relations: *Pedophobic Dog* (fig. 36) and *Cynophobic Child* (fig. 37). Peter produced many images of dogs, observed in all kinds of poses and situations; he gathered some of them into a collection, which he presented to his longtime friend and colleague at Santa Barbara, Alfred Moir, with the pseudo-humanistic title *Cynophilorum Deliciae* (*Delights for Dog Lovers*). A striking image of undomesticated canines, *Wolves in a Forest* (fig. 38), brilliantly uses the twisted forms of trees to convey the sense of an alien wildness.

Peter did many landscapes and produced them in a variety of ways. The design of *Birch Forest* (fig. 39) originated as a stamped print: it was then photocopied in negative onto colored paper, and extensively reworked with correction fluid, so that it, too, expresses a lyrical response to the spectacle of teeming life. Peter enjoyed using stamps to generate the forms of plants and trees: in *Three Trees* (fig. 114), for instance, he employed only a few different stamps, applied in varying positions and configurations, to create the abundant clusters of leaves. Though we may not notice it unless we look carefully, the use of a limited set of basic forms to produce a complex composition creates a distinctive effect, unlike that of the forest scene mentioned earlier: the sense of a simple unity underlying the variety of nature contributes to the satisfaction that we feel as we look. *Landscape with Barren Trees* (fig. 115) is the photocopy of a collage made of black and white paper and what appears to be pieces of gauze. While the leaflessness of the trees indicates wintertime, the contrast between their spiky forms and the large, simple shapes of fields and mountains suggest an inextinguishable vitality and potential for growth.Vitality positively bristles from a *Townscape* drawn in pen and ink (fig. 116), an imaginary composite—or perhaps Platonic idea—of a picturesque Italian hill town, with its cathedral at the top and coffee bar on the plaza at the bottom. Peter also employed stamps to create townscapes, evidently challenging himself to generate entire villages out of the simplest possible arrangements of basic shapes (fig. 118). Hovering on the border, so to speak, between abstract compositions and believable places, they make us realize how susceptible we are to the suggestive power of elementary forms and the rudimentary artistic strategies of duplication and variation.

As one would expect, themes from ancient literature, history, and philosophy figure importantly in Peter's work. He depicted many well-known characters and illustrated many myths and episodes from history, returning to his favorites several times over the course of his career. The classics were living things to him, absolutely essential points of reference in any attempt to make sense of the world, and he tended to see echoes of ancient personalities and stories in the people and events around him. That his classicism naturally overlapped his other interests is shown by the fact that many of his images could be described as classical *tipi* or classical *coppie*, and even when he is depicting a subject not taken from antiquity, his approach to it may be structured by classical habits of thought. The ongoing dialogue in his mind between past and present was a source of serious reflection as well as of comic possibility; his approach to graphic media was inherently ironic, as was his engagement with classical subject matter. Modern art contains many parodies of ancient themes: one thinks, for instance, of Honoré Daumier's hilarious series of prints, *L'Histoire Ancienne* (*Ancient History*), in which Greek and Roman stories are enacted by modern Parisians. Peter was aware of such images and his humor is sometimes similar, but it is usually more subtle, more truly ironic. However funny antiquity can be made to seem in light of modern life, it also offers us things modernity cannot; it remains a touchstone of the good, the beautiful, and the true. Even if we can only know it at a distance, we need it: the perspective it offers us is an antidote to banality and vulgarity, and crucial to our spiritual survival.

One of Peter's earliest extant drawings is an exquisite *Eros* (or *Cupid*, frontispiece), made with a fine-pointed rapidograph on rough Italian butcher paper. Probably drawn in the late '50s or early '60s, it elegantly combines the stylistic sensibility of that time with the spirit of ancient art. Carrying a brazier and brand, rather than the more familiar bow and arrow, the god is shown wearing distinctive leggings that reveal his penis. The image draws on ancient poetic sources, which describe him as both beautiful and dangerous, a

36. *Pedophobic Dog*, photocopy

37. *Cynophobic Child*, photocopy

38. ***Wolves in a Forest,*** **photocopy**

39. *Birch Forest,* photocopy reworked with correction fluid

charming but wayward, unruly boy, looking for mischief. On a different note, celebrations of the pleasures of wine and of the release from inhibition it can induce are also frequent in Peter's work: an example is a stamped *Bacchanal* (fig. 119), an impromptu party where even the goat dances. There are numerous images of centaurs, creatures that, because they are half-human, have always been symbols of the bestial urges at work in human nature. A trim and beguiling *Centauress* (fig. 40) clearly indicates the delight Peter took in the idea of such creatures, the way in which, for him, they embodied the pleasures of a life lived near to the senses and primitive instincts.

The story of the fall of Icarus is well known even today. Peter made numerous illustrations of it: in one (fig. 41), the figure was cut from an earlier photocopied version and glued onto a new sheet; a strip of black paper was then added below it, marked with a few horizontal lines and some touches of correction fluid to suggest a bleak expanse of sea. Reducing the myth to its essentials makes its tragic message emphatic and memorable. Somewhat more obscure is the story of how Nero, having achieved absolute power in the political realm, yet dreamed of success as a singer and actor, only to have it elude him. Peter shows the emperor holding a theatrical mask, which seems to mock him as he contemplates it (fig. 42). Ancient writers made Nero into a symbol of vanity and depravity, but the deeper message of Peter's image is that art can make even the mighty look ridiculous, that excellence in art is more difficult to achieve, more worthy of admiration, and more enduring than power. An image of the goddess Minerva, recognizable by her armor, conversing with a pig (fig. 120), makes little sense unless one knows that the aphorism *sus Minervam (docet)*, "a pig teaches Minerva," was an expression often used by ancient Romans for situations in which an ignorant person presumed to instruct a knowledgable one.

40. *Centauress*, photocopy

Sometimes classical themes are presented anachronistically, with figures dressed in modern clothing. A marker drawing of a man in what looks to be a rumpled business suit, straining to carry a rock, depicts Sisyphus (fig. 43). An early stamped image, with figures in the elegant style Peter cultivated during the '60s, shows a young man in Victorian-era knee breeches pursuing a young woman in a miniskirt. The rays emanating from his head serve to identify the boy as Apollo, while the girl, holding a sprig of leaves in her hand, is Daphne (fig. 121). According to the story, the god became enamored of the unwilling nymph and pursued her, only to have her change into a tree before his eyes and thus remain inviolate. Peter's lyrical treatment translates it into the here and now while preserving its quality as a folk tale. The stamped image of a *Dancing Satyr* (fig. 123) juxtaposes a familiar mythological figure with modern wine bottles to suggest that the enticements of drink, as described, for instance, in the ancient verses of Anacreon and his followers, are still deserving of celebration.

The stamped image of a small boy in Victorian or early-twentieth-century clothing, trailing a toy behind him, might seem at first to be a simple slice of life, but it is identified in one of the folders in which Peter kept versions of it as *Young Poet* (fig. 122). The only indication of its real subject is the winged horse, which refers to Pegasus, the mythic creature whose hoofprints became the source of sacred springs symbolic of poetic inspiration. As often occurs in the work of James Joyce, an ancient motif suddenly appears in the midst of modern life, momentarily causing the two worlds to overlap, and the effect is not just ironic but, to use Joyce's expression, epiphanic. This same principle might operate in reverse, so that the modern intrudes upon the ancient: a vigorously drawn but heavily melancholy image of an ancient Roman with folded hands, labeled, in one of its

41. *The Fall of Icarus*, photocopy reworked with pencil and correction fluid, pasted overlays

42. *Nero*, photocopy

43. *Sisyphus,* marker, watercolor, and correction fluid with pasted overlay

printed versions as *Ovid in Exile* (fig. 4), is probably a self-portrait. Peter sometimes likened himself, forced by circumstance to live in California, to the poet Ovid, condemned to dwell among the barbarous Scythians.

Many of Peter's most appealing images might be described as classical *coppie*. The early Greek philosophers Democritus and Heraclitus were understood as antitypes: it was said that the world provoked one to laughter and the other to tears. Peter's depiction (fig. 44), however droll, is yet the work of someone in whose mind the old pairing is the expression of a meaningful dilemma, someone who recognizes that the state of the world requires us both to laugh and to cry. An encounter between a very unabashed prostitute and a timid-looking client in front of an ancient brothel (fig. 45) is labeled with a motto actually found amid the graffiti of Pompeii: *Hic Habitat Felicitas* (*Happiness Lives Here*).

The story of Ganymede, the beautiful shepherd boy for whom Zeus—usually attracted to women—developed a passionate desire and whom he carried up to Olympus to be his cup-bearer, is the subject of another witty image, originally based on wash and marker drawings (fig. 46). The contrast between the sprawling triangular form of the god, presented frontally, dominating the sheet, and the slender shaft of Ganymede, seen in profile and displaced to the side, makes the differences between their two conditions very emphatic: it transforms the image into a study in the difference between selfish calculation and pure innocence. But though Zeus seems to rule supreme, the expression on his face suggests that his desire for the

44. *Democritus and Heraclitus*, photocopy

45. *Hic Habitat Felicitas,* stamped print

46. ***Zeus and Ganymede,*** **photocopy**

boy is deeply disturbing to his sense of omnipotence, and that Ganymede is in fact the all-powerful one.

Pygmalion was a sculptor, the story goes, who made a statue of an ideally beautiful woman and fell in love with it; he prayed to Aphrodite, goddess of love, to bring it to life, and his wish was granted. Peter's version (title page), which began with stamps but was refined in photocopied form, is one of his most brilliant inventions, capturing the spirit of Greek vase painting even while transforming it in a modern way. The individual figures are vividly characterized but, again, the expressive magic lies in their relation to one another, the manner in which even the space between them seems charged with sexual energy, so that the image as a whole expresses the astonishment of instantaneous mutual attraction. Like this fantasy of the artist's ability to achieve the object of his desire, the relationship between the poet and his muse was also of interest to Peter as a metaphor for the relationship between erotic and artistic inspiration, and he treated it numerous times. In one the poet is a young man whose muse seems to have other things on her mind than poetry and is more of a distraction than a help (fig. 124), while in another, a stamped image (fig. 125), he is presented as a middle-aged, henpecked husband.

Religious themes are also frequent in Peter's work. They are usually treated in humorous fashion, as in *Devil with a Cappuccino* (fig. 48), but *Devil and Angel Dancing* (fig. 49), while certainly amusing, also touches on a more serious theme, the insoluble inextricability

47. *St. Simeon Styletes*, photocopy

48. *Devil with a Cappuccino*, photocopy

49. ***Devil and Angel Dancing***, **marker and correction fluid**

—in life as we know it—of good and evil. A depiction of St. Simeon Styletes (fig. 47), the fifth-century hermit who chose to live atop a column to keep himself from temptation, combines bemusement with a certain admiration for the kind of singlemindedness necessary to reject the world so completely. The *Miracle of St. Nicholas of Bari* (fig. 126) illustrates a story, often depicted in medieval Italian painting, in which a Christian boy is rescued from slavery to a pagan lord by being picked up by the hair and carried home. Peter's version combines a genuine affection for the simple faith that could give credence to such a tale with the delight of a modern surrealist in its sheer absurdity. St. Mary Magdalene (fig. 127), having renounced her life of sin and cast away her jewelry, tries on her halo before a mirror, as if it were simply a new piece of jewelry.

If devils abound in Peter's art, so do angels. Two *Censer-Bearing Angels* (fig. 128), intended to form part of a procession, are characterized as male and female, even though, as Peter well knew, angels are officially sexless. The boy does a double-take as he realizes that the angel behind him is outfitted somewhat differently than himself. In addition to wrapping paper (fig. 130), Peter often made his own Christmas cards, and angels appear in most of them. In two watercolor studies, which must have been painted within seconds (fig. 50), each with only a few inspired brushstrokes, the presences are so charged with energy and yet so pensive and ethereal that they really seem to be visitants from a supernatural realm. Worldly though he may have been, Peter knew what an angel is.

The most pervasive theme in Peter's work is love, and as one might expect of a classicist, there are many images of Eros (or Cupid) and Aphrodite (or Venus). A small stamp of *Eros* (fig. 52) aiming his bow upward, was carefully perfected before being photocopied. Peter returned to this image numerous times, improvising on it, not with further changes to the image itself but by framing it and adding epigraphs. On one occasion, he attached a line from the Greek lyric poet Moschus simultaneously celebrating and lamenting the power of the diminutive god: "His hands are

50. ***Pensive Angels***, **watercolor**

51. ***Tua Sum Nova Praeda Cupido (I am Your New Victim, Cupid)*****, stamped print**

52. ***Eros (Cupid)*****, stamped print**

small but they shoot a great distance." Another time, he added an inscription from the *Greek Anthology* meaning "I will make Love the beginning of my speech" (fig. 53). The custom of adding epigraphs to images is of ancient origin, and during the Renaissance, scholars created *imprese*, or emblems, combining an image with a motto to express things about themselves, their friends, or their patrons. By devising this emblem to declare that love will be the motivation of his words, Peter identifies himself as a poet, and invites us to think of him as one of the many poets who have dedicated themselves to the theme of love. The design might thus be taken to stand as a symbol of his entire artistic enterprise.

A stamp of Cupid readying his bow while a kneeling woman offers her breast as a target (fig. 51) was labeled in another version with a line from Ovid, *Tua sum nova praeda Cupido*, "I am your new victim, Cupid." The mischievous boy of ancient myth also appears in many scenes which, to judge from the clothing of the other figures, are to be understood as taking place in the modern world. A woman leaning against an oak tree listens to Cupid speaking to her from one of the branches (fig. 54). Beyond being a poetic suggestion of the general idea that the beauty of nature can encourage our disposition to love, the image is probably inspired by verses of the Greek poetess Sappho, who wrote in a famous passage of love coming upon her like the wind in a grove of oaks. Sappho's lines suggest that the process is unaccustomed and rather violent; the humor of Peter's treatment lies in the way it is made to seem so quotidian and casual. In another print, Cupid takes the hand of an unprepossessing woman in modern dress (fig. 131): her gesture expresses the disbelief of someone who has given up all thought of finding love; in one labeled version, this print is entitled *Are You Serious?*

The stamped image of a woman walking beside a column while another woman on top of the column, naked and holding a whip, looks down on her (fig. 132), makes little sense unless one knows the odes of the Roman poet Horace and can recall the line *Regina sublimi flagello.* The poet, unhappy at the indifference of

ΑΡΧΗΝ ΕΡΩΤΑ
ΤΩΝ ΛΟΓΩΝ
ΠΟΙΗΣΟΜΑΙ

53. *Eros* (*Cupid*) with inscription (*I Will Make Love the Beginning of My Speech*), photocopy

54. ***Sappho*, photocopy**

the woman he admires, begs Venus to "raise your whip," and give her a single, gentle stroke, just enough to arouse her desire for him.

One of Peter's most beautiful creations depicts *The Worship of Venus* (fig. 55). The goddess is placed atop a column, high above her devotees and the city behind them, standing on an orb to symbolize her universal power. The composition derives from Renaissance depictions of the same theme, but while the style has all the humor of Peter's other stamped images, its symmetry and hierarchical order give it a monumentality that looks back, past the Renaissance examples, to the magnificent opening lines of *De Rerum Natura*, the great philosophical poem of Lucretius that Peter had begun to translate as a young man. Most of the ambitious poems of antiquity begin with an invocation to one or more of the Muses, but Lucretius begins his with a prayer to the goddess of love herself, whom he regards as the source of all life:

> Mother of Aeneas and his race, delight of gods and men,
> Bountiful Venus . . .
> . . . enthralled by thy charms,
> All creatures gladly follow where thou steppest forth
> To lead them . . .
> For thou alone dost govern all things in nature . . .

Since, in these lines, Lucretius also pleads for the help of the goddess in composing his poem, Peter's image should be understood as a similar plea on behalf of his art.

In addition to Venus and Cupid, other mythological figures exemplify the power of love. Harpies, as we have already seen, are one of Peter's favorite symbols of the dangers of sexual attraction. In one of the little paintings on transparent plastic that he subsequently turned into a print, a harpy disguised in modern dress

55. ***The Worship of Venus*****, stamped print**

56. ***Centaur and Lover*****, photocopy**

57. ***Centaur and Lover,*** **photocopy**

beguiles a young business executive (fig. 133). In a more disturbing image, a brutish and angry man, also dressed in modern clothes, seizes a harpy by the wings and prepares to clip them with a huge pair of scissors (fig. 134). Provoking the resentment of those whom they seduce, harpies are figures for the ambivalence of desire. Peter's representations of them, taken together, express a range of emotions that can be assumed to document the range of feelings aroused by his own susceptibility to women, from fascination and delight to pity and rage.

Peter was fond of centaurs, as has already been said, and two versions of the same theme, a male centaur with a human lover, are among his most appealing images. The earlier of the two, photocopied from a stamped image, was probably made in the '60s or early '70s (fig. 56); the second, also from a stamp but reworked with marker, may date from two or three decades later (fig. 57). The pairing between the human and the half-human is bestial, yet Peter makes it seem wholly natural: indeed, the half-animal form of the male partner has the effect of subtly emphasizing the specifically sexual element in the relationship while also suggesting its eventual taming, its elevation into a higher form of love. In the first version, the woman's face is averted, so that her modesty itself seems to be the taming influence. In the second, both faces are turned away, emphasizing the privacy of the shared emotion. The beauty of sexual intimacy has rarely been represented with such tact and tenderness. More comical is the spectacle of a satyr—another half-human creature famous for its sexual appetite—offering his heart: with its combination of sincerity and self-mockery, it makes the perfect Valentine's Day card (fig. 58).

An image of a naked woman riding on the back of an old man refers to a medieval legend involving the ancient Greek philosopher Aristotle (fig. 135). Although the wisest man of his time, Aristotle was so smitten by a woman named Phyllis that he submitted to the humiliation of allowing her to bridle and ride him as if he were a horse. The story remained popular down through the Renaissance as a cautionary example of the power of women: that it exposes the vulnerability of learned men, in particular, is obviously the reason Peter liked it so much. The delightful *She-Devil with Victim* (fig. 136) expresses the same idea, while *Il Conte* (*The Count,* fig. 137) employs a similar device to remind us that Peter also witnessed and sympathized with female victimization.

One of the ways Peter reconsidered and reworked his images involved making inscriptions for them. These

58. ***Be My Valentine!*** **Photocopy**

were sometimes passages from ancient literature, but he also composed many of his own, in Hungarian, in imitation of ancient models. He sent a collection of these prints to his longtime friend, János Szilagyi, giving the volume a long Latin title that makes fun of learned compendia. One of the sheets included in that set derived from a stamped print, representing Cupid tormenting a seated woman with the flames of his torch (fig. 59). The image is eloquent enough without any label, but in one version, Peter added the words *Uritur Infelix Dido*, "unhappy Dido burns," a phrase from Vergil's *Aeneid*. In the version he sent to Szilagyi, however, such an obvious citation was unnecessary, and he replaced it with a comical distych of his own invention.

Other images rely on different kinds of learned references. *Marx and Hegel* (fig. 60) illustrates Marx's claim that he had so radically revised Hegel's conception of dialectic that he had "stood Hegel on his head." In another passage, however, Marx said that he had found Hegel standing on his head and had put him back on his feet. Peter had no end of fun with the mixed metaphor, devising the image in such a way that, hung upside down, it shows Hegel standing on his feet and Marx on his head. In some versions, he put his

59. ***Dido*****, photocopy**

60. ***Marx and Hegel*,** photocopy

monogram on both the "top" and "bottom" of the sheet, so it could be hung either way, and the very idea of top and bottom is called into question. He also did a version with both options on the same sheet and composed an epigraph for it.

Still other motifs have their sources in the visual arts rather than in literature or philosophy. They include the portraits of famous people which, using a Renaissance term, Peter classified under label *uomini illustri* (illustrious men). Renaissance scholars collected portraits of distinguished persons in order to inspire themselves to great achievements; Peter created his own. If we think of them as belonging among his *tipi*, we recognize again how the great cultural legacy he had assimilated through study was a direct extension of his personal experience, how the great men and women of the past were, in a sense, people that he knew. Not all the images from older visual sources are so high-minded, however: a human figure with no head but a face on its rear end, labeled with the pseudo-scientific species designation *Procterocephalus* (fig. 62), was inspired by Renaissance woodcuts of the headless (*acephalic*) people that were believed to live in remote parts of the earth (fig. 61).

As has already been seen in the *Allegorical Figure* (fig. 82) and *Capriccio* (fig. 83), one of Peter's favorite sources was both literary and visual: Cesare Ripa's *Iconologia*, an encyclopedia of allegorical imagery, was first published in 1593 and reissued many times in the seventeenth and eighteenth centuries. Intended to help artists create personifications that would communicate abstract ideas more effectively, it provides descriptions of what such figures should look like; some of the later editions were partly illustrated. It was popular with artists for many generations but is now used mostly by art historians to figure out the meanings of old pictures. That beyond its usefulness for his scholarship, the book inspired Peter's artistic production is an indication of the way in which, for him, abstract ideas were real and meaningful things, vital instruments

61. ***Acephalic Blemmye*, woodcut from the *Liber Chronicarum*, (*Nuremberg Chronicle*), Nuremberg, 1493**

62. ***Procterocephalus*, photocopy**

of the imagination, representatives of a realm where everything is present in clearer, purer, and more perfect form than our ordinary experience allows us to apprehend.

It is fitting that one of the liveliest of Peter's Ripa images is a marker drawing representing *Disegno* (*Drawing*, or *Design*, fig. 63), the fundamental Renaissance value that played such an important role in Peter's own work. Ripa describes *Disegno* as a noble youth, magnificently dressed, holding a mirror and a compass to express the need for sensitivity to visual appearances, on the one hand, and intellectual understanding, on the other. Perhaps the most beautiful of Peter's Ripa's images is *Imaginazione* (*Imagination*, fig. 65): a woman standing with her hands crossed over her breast, wings at her head, and a crown with many tiny figures in various poses. Ripa explains that the wings and crown symbolize the volatility and abundance of the imagination, "whence arise a thousand thoughts and perturbations." Peter follows the model (fig. 64) closely, except that, where Ripa wants the woman to be looking upward toward heaven, Peter

63. ***Disegno*** **(*Design*, after Ripa), pencil and marker**

64. ***Imaginazione*** **(*****Imagination*****), woodcut from Cesare Ripa, *****Iconologia*****, Padua, 1618**

65. ***Imaginazione*** **(*****Imagination*****, after Ripa) photocopy**

shows her with her eyes closed: the effect of blissful, exalted concentration on her inner world, of the quiet strength necessary to quell those thousand perturbations, says a great deal about Peter's experience of his own imagination and what he thought it means to be an artist.

The emblem entitled *Philosophia Duce Regredimur* (fig. 67) was adapted from a Renaissance medal (fig. 66). In its original context, the motto, "philosophy leads us back," means that philosophy guides us back to first principles, to the truth. The figural motif is based on a famous passage in Plato's *Symposium*, in which the power of love is explained with a parable. Originally, the story goes, individual human beings were both male and female, and had two heads, four arms, and four legs. In order to punish them, Zeus decided to split them down the middle: as a result, people are now condemned to wander the earth feeling incomplete until they find their other half. The combination of image and motto on the medal suggests that to seek the truth is to seek that moment when we knew a wholeness that we can only recover in perfect love. Peter changes the anatomy, however, presenting us with a man and a woman attached back to back—in the wrong way—kicking and flailing in the darkness, so that they become a metaphor for all hopelessly unhappy

66. Medal of M.A. Passeri, engraving from G.F. Tomasini, *Elogia virorum . . . illustrium . . .*, Padua, 1644

67. *Philosophia Duce Regredimur* (after Passeri's medal), photocopy

relationships. Even the motto seems to imply something more sinister: it can also be interpreted to mean "philosophy makes us regress," as if our powers of reason do not liberate us from our pain but only make it worse. Although the sources of the emblem are found in ancient philosophy and Renaissance humanism, Peter has interpreted it in a strikingly modern way, so that it might perfectly illustrate one of Freud's darkest insights into human nature, his claim that "however strange it may sound, we must reckon on the possibility that something in the nature of the sexual instinct itself is unfavorable to the realization of complete satisfaction."

Some of Peter's work is devoted to specifically Hungarian themes. He provided illustrations for a translation of the national epic, *János Vitéz* (*John the Valiant*), prepared by his colleague at Santa Barbara, John Ridland, and published in 1999. He also composed what we would now call a graphic novel, *Fasza Miska* (*Mishka the Prick*), a mock-epic about the sordid adventures of a coarse Hungarian rustic. It was never published, but Peter sent a copy to János Szilagyi, as a lowly diversion from all the lofty humanistic interests that they shared. He began to make a series of illustrations for Gyula Krudy's *Álmoskönyv* (*Book of Dreams)* a half-comical guide to the interpretation of dreams that sidesteps Freud's monumental scientific study to draw instead upon folklore and fantasy. The image of an old woman ironing (fig. 21) may have been made specifically for this project, since a printed version bears an inscription from Krudy's text, explaining that a dream about ironing a shirt means imminent engagement. But Peter also seems to have adapted images he had made independently: the watercolor of *Woman Hanging Laundry* (fig. 80) was printed and labeled *To Hang a Tablecloth in a Strong Wind Means Merriment for the Woman*. That the original watercolor was not produced for the Krudy collection is indicated by the fact that in the printed version, the items on the clothesline had to be altered to include a tablecloth. In Krudy's work, Peter seems to have found a way of looking at the world that answered to his own, a way of seeing the dimensions of possible meaning concealed in everyday things and of recognizing the comic potential in the intuition that what we commonly call reality is but the raw material of another reality.

CONCLUSION: STYLE

We usually think of style as a consistent and distinctive appearance that sets the products of one artist apart from those of another. We value that consistency because it reflects a method of working, and beyond that, a way of thinking. Style seems to point beyond itself, or within itself, to something more fundamental. If we understand that it depends on purposeful selectivity—choosing certain things for inclusion and suppressing others in order to achieve a particular look or effect—then we can see that it is a direct extension of the processes involved in any kind of artistic production. That thing to which style points is, in the first place, art itself; style is art emphasizing itself.

Since the decisions that any artist makes in the process of creating something are not just a matter of technical expertise, however, but also of an outlook on the world as a whole, those decisions also point beyond or within themselves to the artist's character, to an internal poise achieved in the process of living. The interest and value of style is thus twofold: its significance as a residue of the work an artist does specifically in making art, on the one hand, and the work involved in reckoning with life and its challenges, on the other. If style is art emphasizing itself, it is also character revealing and emphasizing itself; as such, it has an inherent human interest and moral content.

Peter Meller's work involves different styles, but is also animated by an underlying consistency, and our interest and pleasure in it has to do with our sense of that consistency being something he wanted us to notice, of its being the way his character emphasized itself, and thus testified to the moral significance of his experience. We have noted an ironic humor in his use of graphic techniques, as well as in his relation to classical art and culture. We have glimpsed a sovereign comic outlook on life, most apparent in images that combine objectivity and sympathy. An unresolved tension is evident in his treatment of some erotic themes, and there is a preoccupation with the darker forces at work in human nature, yet even his unresolved tensions are unresolved in consistent ways: there is, we might say, a style to his irony, in which something fundamental about his character, his mode of being, also expresses itself. In some cases we have seen him working through ambivalence to moments of poise, to arrive at formulations in which he seems to get the better of his conflicted feelings, and we sense that the work of making art has helped him do so.

The story of William Tell is Swiss in origin, but it was popular in mid- to late-nineteenth-century Hungary, at a time when, like the Swiss before them, the Hungarians were struggling to free themselves from Austrian domination. The style of Peter's image (cover and fig. 68), looks back to the popular prints of that era; the pleated collar, knickers, and buckled shoes situate the image in the bourgeois world of Victorian children's books. This child of privilege, however, has suddenly awakened to the realization that life is dangerous. He knows that he has had a narrow escape, recalling Peter's own narrow escapes, first from the fascists, then from the communists. To anyone familiar with Hungarian history, the arrow recalls the hated emblem of the Arrow Cross. Though he has been lucky, the boy seems just as nervous as he might have been before the arrow was shot. Perhaps he just now realizes the danger he was in all along, or perhaps he is expecting to be shot at again: once traumatized, the anxiety never goes away. In him, Peter has given us a self-portrait, but also a modern everyman, a symbol of all who live under the threat of violent coercion. He may be a survivor, but he will always be haunted by the terror he has felt.

All the same, the image is comical. Terror and humor are set side by side in perfect ironic reciprocity: dwelling on one, we are never allowed to forget the other. The history of central and eastern Europe in Peter's time is especially rich in memorable examples of the ways in which humor can serve as an antidote to fear. Humor, including ironic humor, can be an expression of the resilience and strength of character necessary to endure the unendurable: it too has inherent moral content. Peter's capacity to objectify himself has already been described as the "hidden rigor" of his comic outlook. In this case, his ability to find a source of amusement even in his own fear exposes something deeper still: the strength of character sufficient to recover an internal poise where—in the face of radically divergent, mutually exclusive emotions—any poise would seem to be impossible. Peter has used his art to get the better of his demons, and to model a style of being that may inspire and guide us in getting the better of ours.

68. ***The Son of William Tell*, photocopy reworked with marker and correction fluid**

69. *Youth with a Book*, pencil

70. *Pan*, pencil

71. *Bureaucrat*, pencil

72. *Very Old Woman*, pencil

73. ***Mermaid with a Mirror*****, marker and correction fluid**

74. ***Man Lighting a Pipe*****, pencil , marker and correction fluid**

75. ***Gyspy Mother***, marker

76. *Two Men Struggling,* marker and correction fluid

77. ***Hedgehog***, **marker**

78. ***Lemur***, **marker**

79. *János in the Forest,* marker and stamps

80. *Woman Hanging Laundry*, watercolor

81. *Béla Bartók*, watercolor and correction fluid

82. *Allegorical Figure* (after Cesare Ripa, *Iconologia*), marker and correction fluid

83. *Capriccio* (*Caprice*, after Cesare Ripa, *Iconologia*), marker and correction fluid

84. ***The Ill-Tempered Clavier***, photocopy

85. ***Woman on a Rock in the Sea,*** **marker**

86. *Woman on a Rock in the Sea*, photocopy

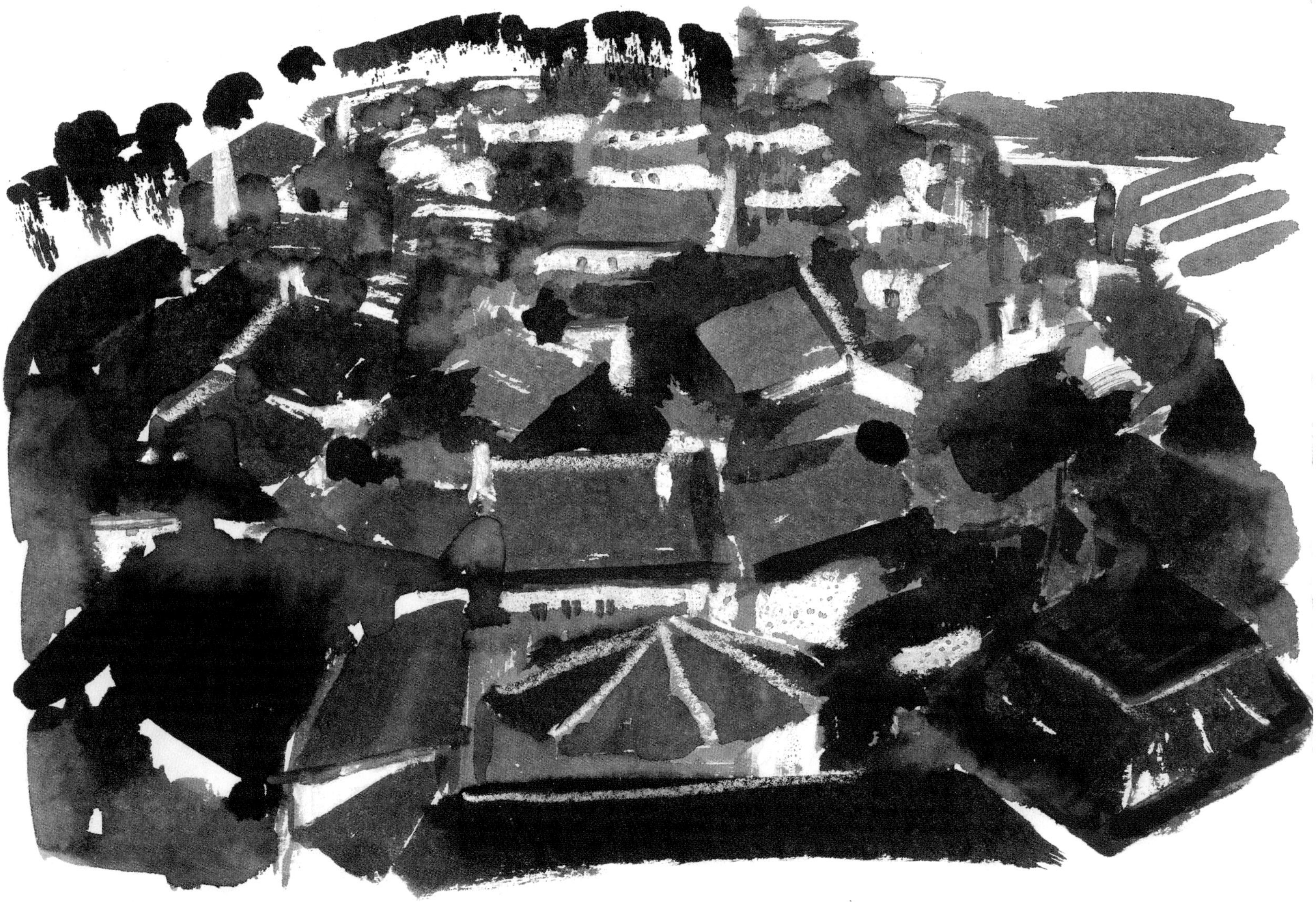

87. *Rooftops*, watercolor

88. *Rooftops*, photocopy

89. *Pandora*, pencil and marker

90. *Pandora*, photocopy reworked with marker and correction fluid

91. ***Seated Girl in Classical Dress***, **photocopy**

92. ***Seated Girl in Classical Dress***, **photocopy on colored paper reworked with correction fluid and oil crayon**

93. ***The Old Pope,*** **photocopy on colored paper reworked with correction fluid and oil crayon**

94. *Old Woman*, pencil and marker

95. *Old Woman*, photocopy

96. *Mermaid*, correction fluid on black paper

97. ***Mermaid***, photocopy on plastic sheet, mounted on colored foil

98. *Venus at her Toilette*, photocopy on plastic sheet, mounted on colored foil

99. *Apollo*, photocopy on plastic sheet, mounted on colored foil

100. *Rogier van der Weyden,* correction fluid on plastic sheet

101. *Albert Einstein,* correction fluid on plastic sheet

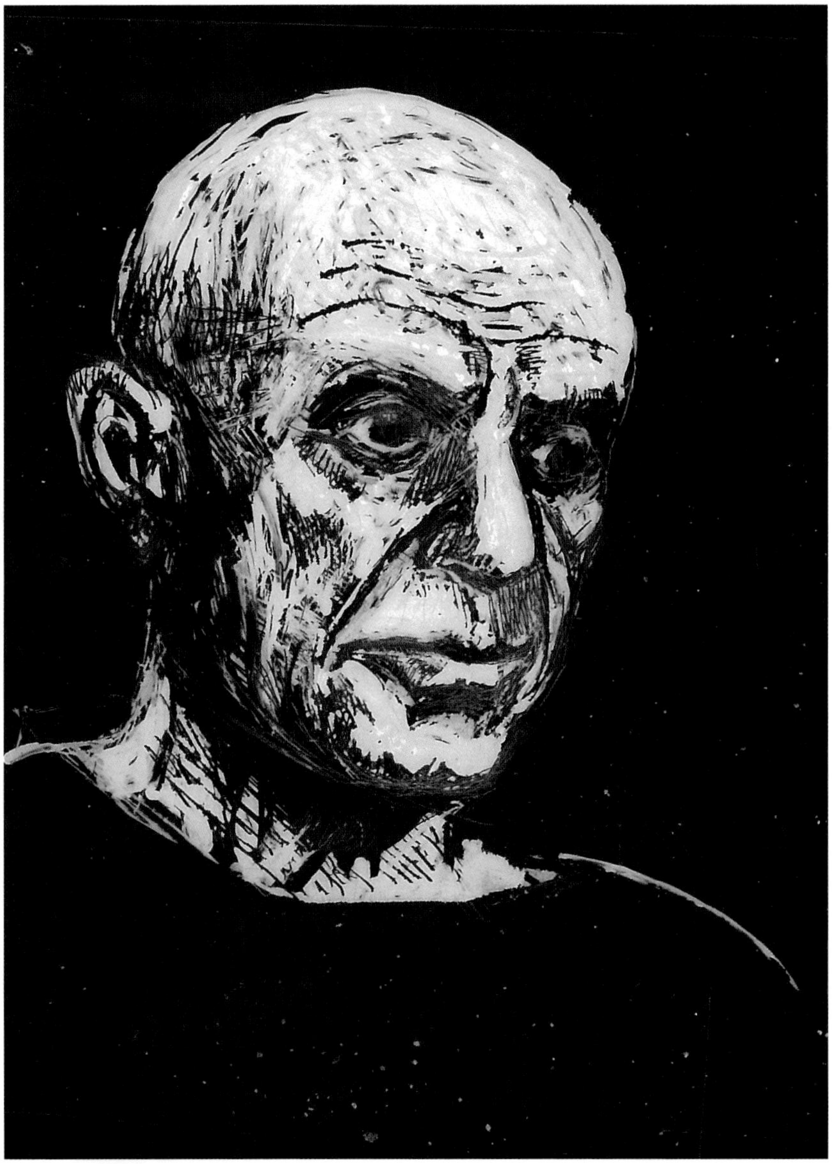

102. *Pablo Picasso*, correction fluid on plastic sheet

103. *Samuel Beckett*, correction fluid on plastic sheet

104. *Pandiramerinaio,* stamped print

105. *Man with Wine Bottles,* marker and correction fluid

106. *Woman with Flowers,* watercolor and oil crayon

107. *Two Women at a Railing*, watercolor

108. ***Couple*****, watercolor**

109. *Unequal Couple*, pencil, watercolor, and correction fluid

110. *Unequal Couple*, photocopy reworked with marker and correction fluid

111. *Gathering Chestnuts*, stamped print

112. *Old Man Scolding a Boy*, pencil and watercolor

113. *Two Men Arguing*, marker, watercolor, and correction fluid

114. *Three Trees*, photocopy

115. *Landscape with Barren Trees*, photocopy

116. *Townscape* (*Italian Hilltop Town*), pen and ink

117. *Italian Village*, styrofoam, cardboard, and paper

118. *Village*, stamped print

119. *Bacchanal*, photocopy

120. *Sus Minervam*, photocopy

121. *Apollo and Daphne,* stamped print

122. *Young Poet,* stamped print

123. *Dancing Satyr,* stamped print

124. *Poet and Muse,* photocopy

125. *Poet and Muse,* stamped print

126. *The Miracle of St. Nicholas of Bari,* photocopy

127. ***St. Mary Magdalene***, watercolor and correction fluid

128. *Censer-Bearing Angels*, stamped print

129. *Angel with a Mandolin*, stamped print > > > >

130. Design for wrapping paper, stamped print > > > >

131. *Are You Kidding?* photocopy

132. ***Regina Sublimi Flagello*, stamped print**

133. *Harpy and Victim*, correction fluid on plastic sheet

134. *Revenge*, photocopy

135. *Aristotle and Phyllis,* photocopy

136. *She-Devil with Victim,* stamped print

137. *Il Conte* (*The Count*), photocopy

ISBN: 0-942006-75-5

Produced for Art, Design & Architecture Museum,
University of California Santa Barbara
by Perpetua Press, Santa Barbara
Typeset in Trebuchet, Kabel and Univers fonts
Designed by Dana Levy
Edited by Letitia O'Connor

Printed in China by Toppan Printing Co.

COVER: *The Son of William Tell*, photocopy reworked with marker and correction fluid

BACK COVER: *Signs of the Zodiac*, photocopy on plastic sheet mounted on color foil

PAGE 1 (frontispiece): *Eros* (*Cupid*), pen and ink

PAGE 2 (title page): *Pygmalion and Galatea*, photocopy

PAGE 4-5 (preface): *Harpy*, printed paper, folded, with jeweler's pins

PAGE 6: *Siren*, stamped print

PAGE 7: *Apollo and the Muses*, stamped print

PAGE 120: *Dioscurides*, watercolor, oil crayon, and marker

ENDPAPERS: *The Signs of the Zodiac*, stamped print